MOSTLY CLIFTON

MOSTLY CLIFTON

IMAGES FROM THE RECENT PAST

Cedric Barker

 *Redcliffe*

First published in 1997 by Redcliffe Press

British Library Cataloguing in Publication Data
A catalogue record for this book is available from The British Library

ISBN 1 900178 11 7

Redcliffe Press,
Halsgrove House,
Lower Moor Way,
Tiverton, Devon EX16 6SS
Tel: 01884 243242
Fax: 01884 243325

Printed by WBC Ltd, Bridgend

Contents

INTRODUCTION
Behind the Camera

I first met Cedric Barker in the early 1960s when I visited his house in Canynge Square to collect photographs for some long forgotten publicity work I was doing for a Bristol client. Some years later, my wife and I found ourselves as near neighbours of Cedric's, and like other parents we commissioned him to take photographs of our growing family. It was during these years, while earning a living as a commercial photographer, that Cedric was quietly recording the streets and buildings – and the people – of the Clifton he loved.

Mostly Clifton comes out of a chance meeting with Cedric and his wife, Kathleen, in 1996. They had left Canynge Square some years earlier for Olveston, and we had lost touch. During my own twenty-five years or so in Canynge Square, I had seen Clifton change, imperceptibly day on day, but quite dramatically when viewed across the decades. How better to record this than in a book of Cedric Barker's photographs? Cedric, with many hundreds of negatives filed away, had been thinking along the same lines. It was a short step to our agreeing to publish a collection of his photographs of Clifton from the 1950s to the late 1970s.

The changing character of Clifton had not been so much in the buildings themselves, although many had been transformed as they were rescued from dereliction; in that rather odious Eighties tag, it was more a matter of changing life-style. One tiny incident from 1972 stays in the memory, when high-flying London friends, who had just launched a pioneering Euro-magazine, were spending a recuperative weekend here. As we strolled down the Mall, our footsteps echoing in the empty street that Saturday evening, they asked 'Is it always as quiet as this?' and ingenuously I had replied 'Of course, Clifton never changes'. But, as we now know, 'Britain's leafiest suburb', in John Betjeman's happy phrase, was about to change for ever. A photograph in this book shows Carwardine's tea and coffee rooms fronting the Downs at the top of the Mall; if one can pin-point the start of the sea-change, the granting of a pub licence when the building changed hands may have been such a defining moment.

Doubtless, the pub developers were pushing at an open door. Clifton could not isolate itself from changing social patterns, even if Bristol's planners seemed to take the view that it could look after itself. The years since Cedric Barker took his first photographs in Clifton have indeed seen big changes in 'the village': gentlemen can no longer be fitted out by John Bedford in Boyce's Avenue, or Steer & Geary in the Mall; there are fewer butchers, hardware merchants, grocers and 'fruit and veg' shops, their places taken by estate agents and building societies, off licences, restaurants and boutiques; the seeming paradox of fewer student flats but many more student cars.

This first published collection of Cedric's work draws largely on images of Clifton from those three decades, but it also includes earlier work. The earliest is of the Prince of Wales, captured on film by the budding schoolboy photographer in 1927, and there are images of a post-war Bristol battered by Hitler's bombs and about to fall before the developers. But most are of Clifton before the coming of commuter cars and the current threat of theme pubs; a Clifton still with echoes of Miss Mole and those other characters who peopled the 'Upper Radstowe' of E. H. Young's delicious novels; of customers chatting in corner shops, of empty streets and still-decayed Georgian gentility. And there are some of Cedric Barker's celebrated images of the Observatory and of Brunel's masterpiece spanning the Avon.

These hundred or so photographs do indeed tell a story and fix for ever how Clifton looked while in transition during the post-war decades, but they are not presented as an exercise in nostalgia. They were chosen by Cedric Barker himself for their intrinsic interest as photographs or because they were particularly satisfying as compositions or elements of design. 'Yes, I was quite pleased with that one' was a refrain which often punctuated our very agreeable sessions together.

Although there is no agenda, the photographs have been grouped in a logical sequence, partly chronological in the early images of Bristol immediately after the end of the Second World War, but in the main topographically, from the city centre and approaching Clifton up the hill from the river, striking to the heart of Clifton village, and concluding with a series of striking images of Clifton's most celebrated showpiece.

Cedric Barker was born in Worcester on 30 April, 1911. Two years later, the family moved to Bristol when his father, then a teacher, was offered a post as curate at St Paul's Church, Clifton. They lived in Belgrave Place, and the young Cedric attended a dame school, joining half a dozen other young children in a front room on Sion Hill.

The family left Clifton in 1917, when Cedric's father became vicar of Bishopston Parish Church, but the young lad moved to the XIV School, then located at 14 Apsley Road, from where he obtained an exhibition to North Town, Clifton College. His time at Clifton, from 1924 to 1929, saw a growing interest in photography. He had first got the bug with an O Brownie camera when eight years old, working up, by 1927, to his first 'real camera', a Thornton-Picard Reflex. It was 'a massive great thing', with which he took the earliest pictures in this collection. The Prince of Wales came to the college, in 1927, to open the new science building. 'We were told we could photograph the event, provided we were discreet,' Cedric

recalled. 'So there I was in the audience, standing up with that enormous black box with a hood; it went off with a great crash, everyone looked round and I felt like a mortified character in an H. M. Bateman cartoon!'

After taking a degree in classics from St Catharine's College, Cambridge, he taught at prep schools in Shrewsbury and Scotland. He enjoyed the experience, but was not a good teacher and returned to Bristol to work in the BAC cost office for a while. Giving teaching another try, he joined the staff at the Cathedral School in 1940, 'where, if anything, I was even less able to control the boys'. His war effort then included two years working in a factory at Lodge Causeway making Orlikon anti-aircraft guns for merchant ships, to be followed by a spell driving a jeep around Bristol delivering mail for the American forces.

After the war, a final, brief return to teaching took Cedric to Bristol Grammar School, where he met Kathleen, who was to become his second wife. She helped him take the plunge into professional photography, at which he 'strugggled on' till 1951 when he received his first big break. His winning entry in the Children's Section of the *Picture Post* photographic competition brought a then substantial first prize of £100, and some useful publicity at a cheque presentation ceremony during a film show at the old Empire Theatre in Old Market. On the strength of this, he bought a new bike and hired a room in Filton Avenue as a studio. 'I took to cycling to the Downs, asking parents if I could take a picture of their children. That was something one could do without embarrassment in those more innocent days.'

The business building up, Cedric and Kathleen married in 1952 and took a basement flat in Hurle Crescent, just off Whiteladies Road. It was fairly basic accommodation, with a disused oil drum as a bath-tub, which before long prompted them to move to something better in Clarendon Road in Redland. Kathleen had become a child care visitor with the City's Children's Department. Cedric was specialising in family and wedding photography, as well as doing contract work for Clifton College and the High School. Daughter Jane was born in 1956, and they bought a house in Canynge Square that year, for the enormous sum of £1600, and where they lived for twenty-eight very happy years.

While living in Canynge Square, Cedric and Kathleen became early members of the Clifton & Hotwells Improvement Society. Cedric took a lot of photographs 'officially' for the Society, but many more for his own interest and pleasure. Three of these were selected by the English judges for entry in Kodak's New York World's Fair 1964-65. One – of a sweet shop in Richmond Terrace with daughter Jane and a friend being served by the proprietor – received the Silver Award, and the other two were awarded bronze medals.

Most of the photographs in this collection were taken using a Rolleiflex camera, and Pentax single lens reflexes. Sadly, Cedric Barker died, in his eighty-seventh year, while the book was in preparation. He had, though, made his final selection in the weeks before his death. When, at our last meeting, I said I hoped I had not tired him unduly, Cedric smiled his lovely smile and murmured 'Not at all, not at all. It has been most stimulating.' So it is good to know that there are no photographs here with which Cedric was not 'quite pleased'; and that **Mostly Clifton** can be offered as a fitting tribute to a fine photographer and a truly gentle man.

John Sansom, August 1997.

The winning Picture Post *photograph.*

Paul Robeson and Dame Peggy Ashcroft.

Bristol in the 1940s and 1950s

The 1950s: when church spires and industrial chimneys still dominated the Bristol skyline.

St Mary Redcliffe, with railway sidings.

Letting sleeping dogs lie in King Street.

Mr and Mrs Shipp happy in their work at the Bristol Old Vic's gallery bar 'in the Gods'.

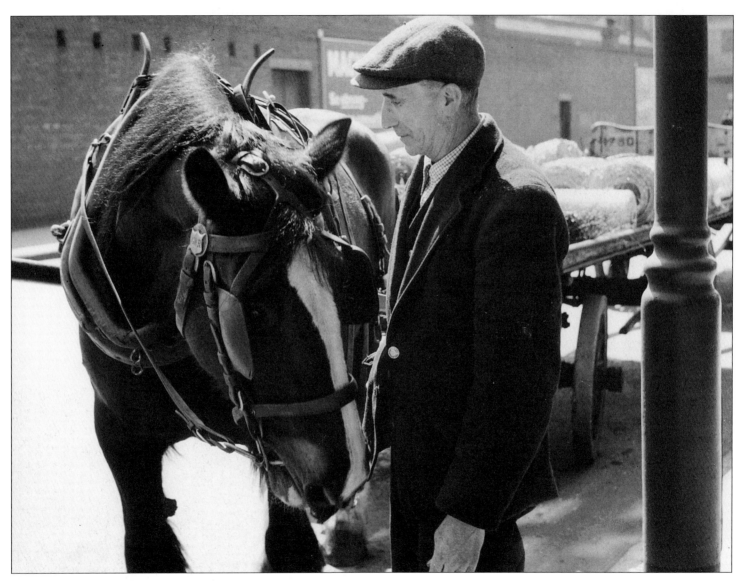

A George's Brewery horse.

A quiet Horsefair just before the construction of the controversial Lewis's Department Store in the mid-1950s.

College Street about to be demolished for municipal car parking behind the Council House.

House proud: a College Street resident.

Bristol for the people: College Green in 1957.

Mrs Penfold from Congresbury: a familiar figure in the city streets.

The Upper Arcade: victim of Hitler's bombs.

The bottom of Christmas Steps before restoration.

Looking down Christmas Steps.

A run-down St Michael's Hill in 1954.

Approaching Clifton

Looking towards Clifton from Rownham Hill in the late-1950s. Trains and few cars.

St Vincent's Parade below the rear of Windsor Terrace.
Campbell's pleasure steamers used to ply from the landing stage.

St Vincent's Parade on Hotwell Road.

The Colonnade: survivor from the glory days of the Hot Well.

Hotwells before the Cumberland Basin flyover and (right) Windsor Terrace before the new flats were built.

Hinton House: photograph taken from a rear window in Freeland Place.

Looking down from Windsor Terrace before the kitchen gardens were built over.
The hillside is across the water on the Somerset side of the river.

Windsor Terrace gate post.

Granby Hill before re-gentrification.

On the way down, but soon to be rescued in the Hotwells revival.

'No Hope' Square was to confound the pessimists.

Jacob's Wells Buildings in the 1950s.   Built in the 1870s by Susannah Winkworth
for the decent poor, they would soon make way for council flats.

Rear of Jacob's Wells Buildings.

Also long since gone: F. Smith's shoe repair shop.   Not to be outdone by the QEH boys, the urchin insisted on appearing in the photograph.

Rock Court, off Berkeley Place, demolished in 1967 for a multi-storey car park. Alice Davis standing at No 2.

Clifton Village

Clifton Road, looking towards the Bishop's House. The buildings on the left were later demolished for student flats. 'Old' Labour was a novelty then: the newspaper placard questions the merits of State control.

Sweetshop at the top of Richmond Terrace.

Christchurch School: now the Clifton Library.

The Arch Pharmacy, Boyce's Avenue.

Mrs Matthews and Nelson, newsagents in The Mall, 1960s.

Mr Baldwin the chemist: the pharmacy on the corner of The Mall and West Mall is still largely unchanged today under a new name.

Mrs Bishop's corner shop in 1964.   Now a jeweller's.

Quintessential shabby-genteel Clifton: Royal York Crescent in the early-1960s.

Clifton Assembly Rooms.

'Not much world news today.'

Clifton Down fountain.

A trudge through Birdcage Walk.

Clifton Downs in the snow.

Making light work of it.

Harley Place.

Genteel luncheons and teas about to give way to 'pub grub'.

A store on every street corner?

Top of the old funicular Rocks Railway.

Crossing the generation gap on Clifton Down.

Looking down Sion Hill.

Waterloo Street in the 1950s.

No need for parking restrictions a generation ago.

(Above) Waterloo Street in the early years of the Clifton Fayre.
(Right) Entente cordiale.

Canynge Square, the College and the Zoo

How did we manage?   Canynge Square without cars.

Canynge Square remains partly gas-lit to this day.

Horse and cart gives way to go-cart in the quiet square.

Communal gardens.

Clifton College network.

The Prince of Wales visits the College to open the new Science Building in 1927, photographed by college boy Cedric.

Another 'snap' by the budding photographer of the visiting Prince of Wales.

Cedric turns sports photographer.

Ouch!

Around the Bridge

Ornamental detail from the Grand Spa ballroom exterior.

More details.

The Observatory observed.

Queuing for the camera.

In the news.

Clifton Down and the Promenade in the snow.

'Here we go!'

The Avon Gorge, attracting sightseers for centuries.

Leigh Woods.

Out for a canter on the Downs.

'Come on, Ted. Before they find us!'

ERECTED BY ALDERMAN THOMAS PROCTOR, OF BRISTOL, TO RECORD THE LIBERAL GIFT OF CERTAIN RIGHTS OVER CLIFTON DOWN MADE TO THE CITIZENS BY THE SOCIETY OF MERCHANT VENTURERS UNDER THE PROVISIONS OF THE CLIFTON AND DURDHAM DOWNS ACTS OF PARLIAMENT, 1861, WHEREBY THE ENJOYMENT OF THESE DOWNS IS PRESERVED TO THE CITIZENS OF BRISTOL FOR EVER.

Victorian philanthropy.

River traffic in the 1950s.

From the Colonnade.

Subscribers

Alice Allred
Vivienne Arengo Jones
John B.C. Arengo Jones
John and Eve Banbury
Mr James Neville Basham
Beryl E. Baverstock, 31 Lynn Road, Snettisham, King's Lynn
Dr and Mrs Colin Bayne-Jardine, Beresford House, 1 Clifton Hill, Bristol
R. L. Bland
E. J. Bland
Alistair Bond
Mrs I. M. Bracegirdle
Jean and Geoffrey Brazier
James Brierley
Lorna Brierley
David Bursey, 28 Queens Road, Westbourne, Bournemouth
Nick Campion
Graham Chapman, 18 South Street, Bedminster, Bristol
Clifton College, 32 College Road, Clifton, Bristol
Clifton Library
Philip Alan Cobb
John and Jennifer Collins
Tony Colman
Frances Conway-Seymour RWA
Mr and Mrs C. R. B. Curtis, The Old Rectory, Kelston, Bath
Mr & Mrs Julia d'Arcy Whitfield
Bill and Sue Dascombe, 13 Canynge Square, Clifton, Bristol
Chris Davis

Mr Jeffrey Davies, 11 Southfield Road, Westbury-on-Trym
Nicky Stuart Davis
Mr and Mrs R.E.H. Davis
Richard Denby
E. J. and H. B. Derrett, 23 Julius Road, Bishopston, Bristol
Anita J. Edouin, 94 Westfield Road, Berkhamsted
Sam and Karen Edwards
John and Joyce Eley
Barbara Evans
Betty and Desmond Fowler
Sue Fowler
David J. Gale
John W. Gallaugher and Sue Arengo
The Goldings
Tom Gover
Marjorie Haskins
Mr and Mrs John Hayes
Eileen Hartly Hodder
Jean and Maurice Ingham
The Kennedy Family
Jane and Paul Kent
Dorothy Irene Kirkham
Beth Langton
Kate Langton
Vic Lawson, Clifton, Bristol
Paul A. Leach
Barbara and Michael Lees
Jennie and Alan Maunder

John and Gillian McKeown
Philip Miles, 11 Clifton Wood Road, Clifton, Bristol
Anne C. Miller
Alwyn B. Miller
H. C. Mitchell MBE
Jessie and Frank Moate, 28 Cliftonwood Crescent, Clifton, Bristol
Michael and Estelle Morgan
Jan Morrison
Mrs M. Page, 12 Upper Berkeley Place, Clifton, Bristol
Nicholas and Pamela Parker
Mr and Mrs Michael Pascoe
Dr Gillian Pengelly
Dr and Mrs C. J. Phillpotts
Philip and Joanna Polack
Gordon and Pamela Priest
Mr E. J. Read, 44 Royal York Crescent, Clifton, Bristol

Anna Rose, 2 Cornwallis Crescent, Clifton, Bristol
John Saunders
N.R.P. Speed
Karen Spencer (née Wilkinson)
John and Di Steeds
Joan Timothy
M.R.C. and J.J. Uren
Bob Vaughan, 3 Pembroke Vale House, Pembroke Vale, Clifton, Bristol
Roy Vaughan
Sue Venning
K. G. Welsford
Harry West, MA, FBATD, ITEC, 23 Tyndalls Park Road, Clifton, Bristol
Marjorie Whicheloe, 7 Camp Road, Clifton, Bristol
Mrs Audrey de Lona White
Joan and Arnold Wynne, 11 High View Close, Chesterfield